John Collyer Knight

The Law, the Prophets, and the Psalms

Their divine Inspiration asserted upon the Authority of our Lord

John Collyer Knight

The Law, the Prophets, and the Psalms
Their divine Inspiration asserted upon the Authority of our Lord

ISBN/EAN: 9783337183462

Printed in Europe, USA, Canada, Australia, Japan

Cover: Foto ©ninafisch / pixelio.de

More available books at **www.hansebooks.com**

"THE LAW, THE PROPHETS,

AND

THE PSALMS:"

Their Divine Inspiration

ASSERTED UPON THE AUTHORITY OF OUR LORD,
AND VINDICATED FROM OBJECTIONS.

WITH

ANIMADVERSIONS IN DISPROOF OF THE TESTIMONY OF
JOSEPHUS IN REFERENCE TO THE CANON.

BY

JOHN COLLYER KNIGHT,

OF THE BRITISH MUSEUM,

AUTHOR OF "THE PENTATEUCHAL NARRATIVE VINDICATED FROM THE
ABSURDITIES CHARGED AGAINST IT BY THE BISHOP OF NATAL," ETC.

LONDON:
LONGMAN & CO., PATERNOSTER ROW.

—

1866.

"THE LAW, THE PROPHETS, AND THE PSALMS."

From the earliest ages of the world down to the days of Malachi, and then, after an interval, from the days of our Lord to the death of the last of his apostles, there has been, according to the admitted facts of Bible history, a succession of men who have at least professed to have received from God instructions and revelations in reference to religious truth. To some extent this was the case even in the days of the patriarchs; indeed, there is reason to believe that it was by revelation to a succession of selected recipients, that religious truth was made known to men from the very beginning. The revelations given, or said to have been given, to these men—to the patriarchs, to Moses, to Samuel, and after them to a long series of prophets—we possess. Are they to be depended upon? Were they inspired?

Inspired or uninspired, the Bible is certainly a very extraordinary book, a very different one from any that has ever been written. No other so recognises God, his rights, his claims, his excellence; no other so speaks to and affects our moral sense of right and wrong; no other seems so divine. And yet, it is not to be denied that, in many respects, it is not what one might *a priori* have expected it would have been. There is in it, for instance, mixed up with much that is of the highest religious importance, much also that religiously is, or appears to be, of no importance at all; and, in so far as this is the case, Scripture, it is argued, cannot be inspired. We are willing to admit the premises. To a certain extent the sacred history, like any other history, is, of course, mere history. Like any other, it treats mainly of the public acts of kings, and warriors, and others. Its authors care as much as other historians to preserve remnants of mere archæology and the like, and to stereotype, by transferring to their pages, in reference to times or persons of whom little was known, such fragments of information or of remembrance as remained; as that "Jubal was the father of all such as handle the harp and organ;" or as that "Tubal-Cain was an instructor of every artificer in brass and iron;" or that Lamech said to his wives as is stated; and to record, as in their estimation worthy of being preserved, many facts and circumstances that in a religious respect were, or seem to have been, altogether valueless. If, then, the end contemplated by the histories of Scripture was simply to make known religious truth, there would be force in the objection. But this was not the case. Facts prove that it was not. As histories, their main and direct end was simply to make known or to perpetuate the remembrance of the events of the times of which they treat. Their religious instruction, in consequence, is, and must be for the most part, only incidental and only occasional. Their peculiarity, as compared with other histories, consists not in that all their details convey moral or religious instruction, but in that when they do convey such instruction, the instruction conveyed is the result of the divine enlightenment of the writers of those histories, and, therefore, truthful and authoritative. Admitting, then, the premises of this objection, we deny the inference.

But it is further objected that duplicate accounts of one and the same event occasionally so differ, or seem so to differ, the one from the other (not, perhaps, in their main features, but in some one or two small particulars, such as the locality of an incident, or the name or names of the party or parties concerned in the same, or some such small matter), as to beget the suspicion that if the one account be strictly accurate, the other cannot be so too. Discrepancies of so trivial a character of course leave unaffected the substantial truthfulness of the narrative, and, in themselves considered, are of small importance; but then, it is argued, discrepancy of statement, however minute and unimportant in itself, is inconsistent with inspiration; and that the writings, therefore, in which such discrepancy is found, whatever their value as a whole, and as the production of honest and well-intentioned men, cannot be inspired.

The latter of these two charges is ordinarily met by a denial that the alleged inaccuracies exist (which denial, as the text now stands, facts will not warrant), or by an assumption that the inexactnesses in question are the fault of a corrupted text. But with a view to the refutation of the inference based upon them, we assume, in reference to each of these charges, that the case is as stated, viz., that in the histories of Scripture there is at times a certain looseness of statement, a certain neglect of strict, rigid literality, a certain measure of inexactness; and that there is, or seems to be, unimportant and uninstructive narrative. For though there can be no question that Scripture has not unfrequently been charged with contradictions, and inconsistencies, and inutilities, groundlessly, it is no less certain that there are instances in which one who in the main believes, or is disposed to believe, in the inspiration of Scripture, is sorely perplexed by at least the appearance of them. To relieve one thus perplexed—not to reply to the objections of the determined, willing sceptic—is the object of these pages. As the basis of our remarks, then, we assume that there are, or seem to be, such narratives, and such discrepancies. Most, if not all of them, may, we believe, be satisfactorily accounted for and vindicated; but, upon the supposition that they cannot, that we have occasionally real discrepancies, positive contradictions, conflicting accounts of one and the same event, useless narratives, or anything else that may be thought to be incompatible with inspiration, does it follow that the books in which they are found cannot therefore be inspired? May not the reality of the discrepancy, or the non-importance of the narrative, be admitted, without impeachment of the inspiration of the writings containing them? We believe that it may.

In the first place, a writer or a book may clearly be inspired in one respect—in a religious, for instance—and not in another. Now Scripture, if inspired at all, is of course inspired in reference to what it tells us of God. Its non-inspiration in other respects, whether apparent only or whether real, whether suspected only or whether proved, can be no disproof of its inspiration in this. It may be that, here and there, some small inexactnesses of minor, petty detail meet us—some unimportant non-accuracy as to the locality or date of an event—or some other one or two of those thousand things to which, through human infirmity, a writer may be liable. But if that which it tells us of God, of God's will, and of God's purposes, and of God's attributes, and of God's character, it tells us because upon these points its writers were divinely instructed and divinely enlightened, then the book must be, is inspired, whether there be in it also human infirmity or not. To say that its teachings upon these points are the result of divine enlightenment, and to say that the book is inspired, is indeed to say one and the same thing. The two propositions are identical.

To prove that it is inspired in this respect, I make no attempt. This I assume; chiefly upon the authority of our Lord. Other and more critical, and, as some may think, more satisfactory reasons, might be assigned for the belief, but to me this is sufficient; and it is sufficient also for the object contemplated by the present essay; which is not to prove the inspiration of Scripture, but, assuming that, to set aside the objection to its inspiration arising from the discrepancies and contradictions upon unimportant non-religious matters, and certain other objections named above, which, whether truly or falsely, have been urged against it.

To suppose, as has been done, that our Lord, in quoting or referring to the writings of the Old Testament as "Scripture," or as the "word of God," spake either in ignorance, or simply out of deference to popular opinion, cannot be admitted for one moment. As regards the supposition that he spake in ignorance, it is true that we are told that the wisdom of the child Jesus, like that of any other human being, increased with his years (Luke ii. 52). But his increase in wisdom is no proof that he was not always wise up to the point that the occasion required. As a child, the same kind and the same amount of wisdom was not requisite as when, in the maturity of manhood, he became a public teacher; nor the same mental power.* But his recognition of the writings of the Old Testament was not the recognition of a child,

---

* "It is perfectly consistent with the most entire belief of our Lord's divinity, to hold that when he vouchsafed to become a Son of Man he took our nature fully, and voluntarily entered into all the conditions of humanity, and, among others, into that which makes our growth in knowledge gradual and limited. With St. Luke's expression before us, it cannot be seriously maintained that as an infant or young child he possessed a knowledge surpassing that of the most pious and learned adults of his nation upon the subject of the authorship and age of the different portions of the Pentateuch. At what period, then, of his life upon earth is it to be supposed that he had granted to him, as the Son of Man, supernaturally, full and accurate information on these points? Why should it be thought that he would speak with certain divine knowledge on this matter more than upon other matters of ordinary science or history?"—"The Pentateuch, &c. examined," by Bishop Colenso, Preface, xxxi.

but of a full-grown man, upon whom, at baptism, the Spirit had visibly descended—to whom that Spirit was "given without measure," whose "words" were "the words of God" (John iii. 34)—who taught, not as the scribes, but "as one who had authority."

If, when a child even, he was "filled with wisdom" (Luke ii. 40), and if thenceforth he "increased in wisdom" (ver. 52), surely when he had attained full manhood, his recognition of these writings is of more worth than our own private judgment, or than the private judgment of any man, episcopal or non-episcopal.

We read that if there be faith in Christ as a Saviour, there shall be salvation. I can conceive it to be possible, therefore, for a man to profess this faith, and even to have it, and yet to doubt as to the full inspiration and strict accuracy of certain of the Old Testament writings;* but it does seem hardly consistent with Christianity to doubt of their inspiration altogether, or of their general and substantial truthfulness—especially with regard to those books (the Pentateuch, for instance, or the Psalms, or the writings of the Prophets) which

* See extract from *Birks* given in *Appendix*.

our Lord and his apostles so often quote or refer to as Scripture. It would perhaps be harsh to say that a man cannot be a Christian who has these doubts; for he may, perhaps, by some subtle reasoning or hypothesis, reconcile them consistently with his faith in Christ as a Saviour. Still, the doubts and the belief do seem not to hold well together. If our Lord be mistaken upon the point, the writer, for one, can have no faith in him in other respects, and is a sinner without a Saviour.

But to proceed with our argument. Non-inspiration in one respect is, we have said, no proof of non-inspiration in another. Non-inspiration, then, in regard to such unimportant details as the precise date or the exact locality of an occurrence (supposing Scripture to have been sometimes inexact in such small matters), is no proof that it was not inspired in reference to religious truth. If the religious teachings of the Bible were meant to be authoritative; if, as a standard of doctrinal and didactic truth, it was meant to be decisive, trustworthy, infallible, and binding, it was of course necessary that upon all religious points it should be divinely inspired. But it was not, upon religious grounds, needful that its inspiration should extend beyond its religious element—except, perhaps, for this reason, viz., that if found to be not inspired in other respects also, men—some men at least—might possibly reject it in the mass, and deny or doubt whether it was inspired at all. And this men do. But it may be that such a possibility was contemplated, foreseen, designed; that God willed that there should be this ground of offence, this difficulty, this stumbling-block, this test of sincerity and earnestness. Truth is seldom attested by overwhelming evidence—seldom compels assent. Probabilities may be in its favour—may preponderate—but there may be circumstances notwithstanding that may induce some to doubt its truthfulness, and to withhold, in consequence, a hearty, full acceptance of it. And if that which is true they wish to be untrue, they will do this, glad to find in those circumstances what they will regard as a justification of their unbelief.

Such a ground of offence, then, may have been designed. It would be but one probation out of the many by which in this state of probation we are surrounded and tested.

But, it may be asked, does not the assertion that *all* Scripture is given by inspiration of God, prove the inspiration of Scripture, not in religious respects alone, but in every respect? No; it does not. For what is—not the forced, but the fair meaning of the words, "all Scripture"? — every word, every sentence, every small detail, every unimportant narrative? or, every Book? The words are as susceptible of the latter of these two senses as of the former. Whether, therefore, they are to be understood in the one, or whether in the other, must be determined upon other grounds than those furnished by the phrase itself. If upon independent grounds there is reason for believing that every word and every narrative of Scripture is alike inspired, then we must of course accept the words in the former of these senses; but if, upon independent grounds, we have reason to believe that the inspiration of Scripture is restricted to its religious teachings, then not only will the words admit grammatically of the sense in which we understand them, but they will even demand it. And if so, then the declaration that *all* Scripture is inspired asserts, not the inspiration of every separate narrative, and of every separate sentence, but the inspiration upon religious matters of every Book—of the historical no less than of the prophetical and doctrinal, and of the prophetical and doctrinal no less than the historical.

With regard to the translation in this passage of the word θπνευστος, "*given* by inspiration of God," we have a further remark to make, viz., that such translation is not exact. It goes beyond the original. It implies, or seems to imply, what the original does not imply. The word "given" suggests something like a continuous dictation, or suggestion, or something of that sort. But the translation is paraphrastical, not literal. The Greek word is more literally translated if "given" be omitted; that which it asserts being not the divinity and authority of all Scripture as *given* by inspiration of God, but its divinity and authority as *being* by inspiration of God. I prefer, therefore, to say that all Scripture is "*by* inspiration of God" than to say that it was "*given* by inspiration of God."

But, leaving these general remarks, there are certain of these books that demand a more especial notice.

As regards that of the Psalms, the imprecatory passages contained therein are very commonly urged in disproof of its inspiration; and to most Christian minds these passages have always presented more or less of difficulty. "Give them according to their deeds; render to them their desert" (xxviii. 4). "Let death seize upon them, and let them go down quick into hell (*Sheol, i.e.,* the grave, or the unseen world); for wickedness is in their dwellings, and among them" (lv. 15). "Be not merciful to any wicked transgressors. Consume them in thy wrath, consume them, that they may not be" (lix. 5). "Persecute them with thy tempest, and make them afraid with thy storm. Let them be confounded and troubled for ever; yea, let them be put to shame, and perish" (lxxxiii. 15, 17). These, it is granted, are very fearful passages; but they are, after all, at least so we think, not so incapable of vindication as some may imagine. We rest our vindication of them not upon the mere fact that the impiety of those against whom they were directed was great and defiant, and their cruelty fierce and bloody; nor upon the mere fact that the evil imprecated was merited; but upon the fact that these imprecations are *in strict keeping with the character of God's ordinary course of action under the Old Testament dispensation.* Under that dispensation, his proceedings, whether as regards his own people or the nations immediately around them, were, in reference to sin, to gross sin especially, marked by a severity which, under the reign of the Messiah, no longer exists. The Israelites transgress in the matter of the golden calf; and the command goes forth, "Put every man his sword by his side, and go in and out from gate to gate throughout the camp, and slay every man his brother, and every man his companion, and every man his neighbour." The Canaanites having exhausted God's long-suffering, and filled up the measure of their iniquities, the Israelites are commissioned (or commanded rather) to extirpate them utterly. "Thine eye shall not pity nor thy hand spare, but thou shall utterly destroy them; both man and woman, infant and suckling, ox and sheep, camel and ass;" and "cursed be he that doeth the work of the Lord deceitfully." It seems as if a dispensation of unsparing severity was a necessary preliminary to one of mercy and long-suffering—as if, without it, men would altogether refuse to believe that God so hated sin as very much to care for it, or as to be willing or disposed to punish it very severely. Under the Old Testament dispensation, therefore, not only was temporal punishment God's ordinary course in reference to the flagrantly impenitent, but that punishment also for the most part was stern, severe, relentless; and included in its fell swoop (in order the more vividly to mark the reality and intensity of the indignation against the sin that had provoked it) not the sinner himself only, but all that appertained to him. This was terrible; but it taught a lesson; and that lesson, if we will learn it, it teaches us to this day.

For not being like-minded with God in this respect, Saul moreover is rejected, and Achan dies; whilst Jehu, for his vigorous execution of God's will in reference to the worshippers of Baal, though "he took no heed to walk in the law of the Lord" in other respects, is commended; and David, for his like-mindedness in the matter, is declared to be "a man after God's own heart."

The ordinary character of God's dealings in

these respects had so associated in the Jewish mind the ideas of flagrant transgression and of flagrant punishment, that the existence of the one appears to have suggested at once, and as it were naturally, the expectation of the other. In the case of gross impiety no other issue seems to have been thought of; so that when the pious among them witnessed persistency in impenitence, and cruel wrong and sin, no other course seemed open to them but to pray that the impenitence and sin in question might meet with their deserved reward, and that the wicked doer of the same might be destroyed.

In the case, then, of those against whom these imprecations were directed, we may without difficulty believe that God, willing their destruction, prompted the prayers in question. There is no need to assume personal vindictiveness for personal injury. The flagrancy of the impiety of those denounced, taken in connection with the fact, that to visit flagrant transgression with stern, unsparing, flagrant punishment, was then God's ordinary course, is quite sufficient to account for these terrible imprecations, without any such gratuitous supposition as that the petitioner was actuated by personal vindictiveness; quite sufficient to warrant the belief that they were prompted not by a spirit of revenge on account of personal wrongs, but inspired by God's own Spirit, as much so as any other of the petitions of the Psalms.

It is idle to allege that Christianity inculcates a different spirit; that the Christian is called upon to bless them that curse him, and to pray for them that despitefully use him and persecute him; and that Christian pity would prompt rather a prayer that the wicked, however wicked, may turn from their wickedness and live. As under the Old dispensation God revealed himself chiefly as severe to punish, so under the New he reveals himself chiefly as ready to forgive. And as under the Old he required of his people the entertainment of sentiments and feelings in reference to gross sin that should be consonant with his own, so under the New he requires a corresponding consonance. No Christian man, consequently, would be justified in so denouncing his enemies as David did: neither, on the other hand, might David innocently pity those whom God had denounced, or bless those whom he had cursed.*

Should it be thought by any one that these remarks are not sufficient to set aside the objection urged, upon the ground of these passages, against the Psalms, no Christian man can hesitate to believe, if upon no other authority, upon that of our Lord, that the Psalms are inspired in some respect. Upon the supposition, then, that they were not inspired as regards these imprecations, it will not follow that they were not inspired as regards the de-

---

* To suppose, however, as men for the most part do, that the command to love one's enemies, to return good for evil, not to avenge oneself, and the like, is peculiar to the gospel, is a mistake. The like command is as plainly given under the Old economy as under the New. "If thou meet thine enemy's ox or his ass going astray, thou shalt bring it back to him. If thou see the ass of him that hateth thee lying under his burden, thou shalt surely help him" (Exod. xxiii. 4, 5). "Thou shalt not avenge nor bear grudge against the children of thy people, but thou shalt *love thy neighbour as thyself*" (Lev. xix. 18).

It is true that our Lord, in his Sermon on the Mount, says, "Ye have heard that it hath been said, Thou shalt love thy neighbour, and *hate thine enemy*," but the words, "and hate thine enemy," are clearly a Jewish gloss. In the Old Testament itself no such addition to the command to love one's neighbour, is anywhere to be met with. In it, vindictiveness upon personal grounds is as much condemned as in the New.

votional spirit and language that pervade them, nor as regards the predictions so wonderfully accomplished in our Lord's life and passion. But, for our own part, we believe that the consonancy of the passages objected to with God's ordinary course of action, in reference to flagrant impenitence under the Old Testament dispensation, sufficiently vindicates the belief that they were as much inspired as any other portion of the Psalms.

In some cases these passages will admit of special vindication upon the ground of misconception or mistranslation; as in Ps. cix.; lxix. 27; cxxxvii. 8, 9; xli. 10; lxxix. 6: but even upon the supposition that they will not, it still remains true that we have our Lord's authority for asserting their inspiration, at least in some respect, and that non-inspiration in one particular is no disproof of full inspiration in another.

The grounds, founded upon the nature of their contents, upon which the inspiration of the Song of Solomon and Ecclesiastes have been questioned, are so well known that it is needless to repeat them. Next to them, perhaps, no books of the Old Testament have been more strongly objected to than the two Books of the Chronicles, chiefly upon the ground of the constantly recurring differences of statements in them from those given in the parallel accounts of Samuel and Kings. These, though none of them are of any practical importance, are certainly very remarkable, as the subjoined instances will show, and at the same time very numerous. We subjoin a few of the more obvious ones:

2 Sam. xxiv. 9.—" And Joab gave up the sum of the number of the people unto the king; and there were in Israel *eight hundred thousand* valiant men that drew the sword; and the men of Judah were *five hundred thousand men.*"

1 Chron. xxi. 5.—" And Joab gave the sum of the number of the people unto David; and all they of Israel were a *thousand thousand and a hundred thousand* men that drew sword; and Judah was *four hundred three score and ten thousand men that drew sword.*"

2 Sam. xxiv. 24.—" So David bought the *threshing-floor and the oxen for fifty shekels of silver.*"

1 Chron. xxi. 25.—" So David gave to Ornan *for the place six hundred shekels of gold.*"

[As regards these two passages, it is possible, indeed, that the " *threshing-floor* " and " *the place* " are not identical.]

1 Kings vii. 15.—" For he [Solomon] cast two pillars of brass, of *eighteen cubits high.*"

2 Chron. iii. 15.—" Also he made before the house two pillars of *thirty and five cubits high.*"

1 Kings vii. 26.—" And it [the molten sea] contained *two thousand baths.*"

1 Kings ix. 28.—" And they came to Ophir, and fetched from thence gold, *four hundred and twenty talents*, and brought it to King Solomon."

2 Kings ix. 27.—" And he [Ahaziah] *fled to Megiddo, and died there.*"

1 Kings xv. 32, 33.—" In the third year of Asa, King of Judah, began Baasha to reign over all Israel in Tirzah, *twenty* and *four* years. And there was *war* between Asa and Baasha, King of Israel, all their days."

1 Kings xxii. 43.—" And he [Jehoshaphat] walked in

2 Chron. iv. 5.—" And it [the molten sea] held *three thousand baths.*"

2 Chron. viii. 18.—" And they went with the servants of Solomon to Ophir, and took thence *four hundred and fifty talents* of gold, and brought them to King Solomon."

2 Chron. xxii. 9.—" And they caught him [Ahaziah], for he was hid in Samaria, and *brought him to Jehu:* and when they had slain him, they buried him."

2 Chron. xiv. 1, 6.—" In his [Asa's] days the land was *quiet* ten years.—He had no war in those years."

xv. 19.—" And there was *no more war* unto the five and thirtieth year of the reign of Asa."

xvi. 1.—" In the *six and thirtieth year* of the reign of Asa, Baasha, King of Israel, came up against Judah, and built Ramah," &c.

2 Chron. xvii. 6.—" And his [Jehoshaphat's] heart

all the ways of Asa his father; nevertheless, the high places were *not taken away.*"

2 Kings xvi. 20.—"And Ahaz slept with his fathers, and was buried *with his fathers* in the city of David."

1 Kings xxii. 48.—"Jehoshaphat made *ships of Tharshish* [*i.e.* 'large merchant vessels'—Davidson] *to go to Ophir* for gold; but they went not; for the ships were broken at Ezion-geber."

2 Sam. x. 18. — "And David slew the men of *seven hundred* chariots of the Syrians, and forty thousand *horsemen.*"

was lifted up in the ways of the Lord; moreover *he took away* the high places and groves out of Judah."
[Possibly this verse has reference solely to the beginning of his somewhat long reign ; see chap. xx. 33, which agrees with Kings.]

2 Chron. xxviii. 27.— "And Ahaz slept with his fathers, and they buried him in the city, even in Jerusalem : but they brought him *not into the sepulchres of the kings of Israel.*"

2 Chron. xx. 35-37.—"And after this did Jehoshaphat join himself with Ahaziah, to make *ships to go to Tarshish* ; and they made the ships at Ezion-gaber. And the ships were broken, that they were not able to go to Tarshish."

1. Chron. xix. 18.—"And David slew of the Syrians *seven thousand* men which fought in chariots, and forty thousand *footmen.*"

1 Kings v. 15, 16.—"And Solomon had three score and ten thousand that bare burdens, and four score thousand hewers in the mountains, besides *three thousand and three hundred* which ruled over the people that wrought in the work."

2 Chron. ii. 2.—"And Solomon told out three score and ten thousand men to bear burdens, and four score thousand to hew in the mountain, and *three thousand six hundred* to oversee them."

Most of these discrepancies may doubtless be accounted for upon the supposition of a corrupted text. Dr. Davidson's remark that "the assumption that there is an error in the text, wherever there is something that is [otherwise] inexplicable, or improbable, or exaggerated, implies a theory of inspiration which overrides existing phenomena" ("Introduction to Old Testament," ii. 114)—a remark which covertly implies that, at least in some instances, the text is not corrupted, but originally incorrect—may be quite true; for the supposition of a corrupted text will, of course, solve all discrepancies. Nevertheless, there is certainly an *a priori* probability that the text of Scripture, no less than that of other ancient writings, would suffer from transcription; and a yet further probability, judging from appearances, that it has so suffered. Almost all the discrepancies that can be accounted for only by supposing a corrupted text, have respect to proper names, or numerals; and these, as Stuart remarks, are plainly the most liable of all things to error on the part of copyists; and "if," as he remarks in continuation, "it could be shown that the older Hebrew MSS. designated numbers by alphabetical letters, as the later Hebrew does, it would be very easy to make out the probability of error in transcription, and to account for it. But inasmuch as this, though often assumed, has never been rendered very probable, we must content ourselves with the not improbable supposition that at least some of the errors in question have arisen from transcription or unskilful reduction. In such a case as that of the age of Ahaziah (who, according to 2 Chron. xxii. 2, succeeds his father at the age of forty-two, instead of twenty-two, as in 2 Kings viii. 26,—a statement which makes him two years older than his father who had just died at the age of forty, 2 Chron. xxi. 20) it would be preposterous to suppose that the error came from the pen of the original writer, for it would prove him to be destitute of common sense; a position which the rest of the book will not permit us to maintain."—"Defence of the Old Testament Canon," page 152.

"But," continues Dr. Davidson, "why should transcribers and others have been so very careless in the Books of Chronicles, compared with the other Scriptures? Why should corruptions be accumulated there, and not elsewhere? Is it not an obvious improbability that there should be a very great disproportion between the corruptions in Chronicles, and those in the other books."—"Introduction to Old Testament," ii. page 114.

Here again, the implication is, that at least some of the differences of statement contained in these books from those given in Samuel and Kings, are possibly not corruptions of a text that was originally correct, but original inaccuracies on the part of the compiler or author of these books. But we have no right to suppose that the vitiated text is always that of Chronicles—never that of Samuel, or of Kings; on the contrary, sometimes, as Dr. Davidson himself elsewhere remarks, the reading of the Chronicles is apparently the correct reading, and that of its parallel in Samuel or in Kings the incorrect; as in 2 Chron. ii. 17, where the overseers appointed by Solomon to superintend his 180,000 workmen are given as 3,600, *i.e.*, one to every fifty; whereas in 1 Kings v. 16, their number is 3,300—a number which will not admit of a like even subdivision. Suspicious excesses of statement in reference to numbers, also, though more frequent in Chronicles than, perhaps, in Samuel and Kings, sometimes belong to these latter books and not to the former. For example, the 800 of 2 Sam. xxiii. 8, are 300 in Chronicles (1 Chron. xi. 11); the 500,000 of 2 Sam. xxiv. 9, are, in Chronicles (1 Chron. xxi. 5), 470,000; and the 40,000 stalls of 1 Kings iv. 26, are, in Chronicles (2 Chron. ix. 25) only 4,000. It would indeed be strange, and no less suspicious than strange, if the corrupted text was always that of the Chronicles, never that of Samuel or Kings; but this is not the case; that it is not, is evident from these instances.

Some of these discrepancies are, however, discrepancies more in appearance than in reality, and may be satisfactorily harmonized without any such supposition as that of a corrupted text.

For instance, in 2 Kings xxi. 4, 5, we are told of Manasseh that " he built altars in the house of the Lord, and altars for all the host of heaven in the two courts of the house of the Lord;" and these altars, according to the Book of Kings, appear to have been left standing up to the eighteenth year of Josiah, the second in succession from Manasseh, who, it is said, "did beat down the altars which Manasseh had made in the courts of the house of the Lord, and cast the dust of them into the brook Kidron" (xxiii. 12). But in the Book of Chronicles Manasseh is represented as having *himself* removed them, repenting of his sin. "He took away," it is said, "the strange gods, and the idol out of the house of the Lord, and all the altars that he had built in the mount of the house of the Lord, and in Jerusalem, and cast them out of the city, and repaired the altar of the Lord" (2 Chron. xxxiii. 15). The Chronicles, therefore, which represents Manasseh as having *himself* removed these altars, seems to contradict the Book of Kings, which represents them as still standing in the days of Josiah.

But he may have done this though nothing is said of it in the Book of Kings. The account there given does not say that he did not; he may have done it, therefore, and yet these altars may still have been standing in Josiah's time. We have only to suppose that Manasseh having removed them, his successor, Amon, of whom it is said that "he served the idols that his father had served," restored them. There is nothing at all improbable in such a supposition, especially as the manifestness of the apparently palpable contradiction between the Kings and Chronicles in this matter, is rather a reason for believing that in some way or other both accounts are correct. With the Book of Kings before him, the later writer, the compiler of the Chronicles, would hardly have ventured upon a statement apparently so at variance with the account there given, were not his own trustworthy.

Of a like character is the apparent conflict between 2 Chron. xiv. 1, xv. 19, and 1 Kings xv. 32—the latter telling us that there was war between Asa, King of Judah, and Baasha, King of Israel, "all their days;" whilst the former tells us that there was almost none at all. But we cannot perceive that there is any necessity that we should understand the expression, "there was war between them all their days," as denoting positive and active hostilities. It may simply denote that the rebellion of Israel against the house of Judah still continued.

But even upon the supposition that these discrepancies cannot be thus harmonized, that they cannot in any way be harmonized, and that the text is not corrupted, it is but natural that one should still hesitate to call in question, in consequence, the inspiration of a book that has been received as inspired ever since the days of Josephus, and perhaps, though not certainly, by our Lord himself. For, although after the destruction of Jerusalem, it was, as we know from Josephus, regarded as inspired Scripture, there is no evidence to show that it was so regarded before his time (as we shall see hereafter) —none therefore that it formed any part of " the Prophets " recognised by our Lord. We do not say that it was not so regarded, but simply that there is no evidence to show that it was. It is not impossible, therefore, that it may have been preserved and valued, not because regarded as equally inspired with the books of Samuel and Kings, but as preserving together with matter that was not from inspired sources, much also that was, and which, but for it, would have been wholly and irrecoverably lost.

But however this may be, of this we may feel sure, viz., that if the book was inspired, its inaccuracies were not; they—cannot have been of God. If inspired, then, it can have been so only in reference to its religious element, in that its religious teachings are the teachings of one, whoever it was that wrote or compiled it, that was divinely enlightened as to religious truth, and divinely qualified to make known that truth to others. And this we believe to have been the case; non-inspiration in a lower respect being clearly [not incompatible with full inspiration in a higher.

Some indeed may think it a very improbable supposition that a writing should be inspired in one respect and not in another; but, in itself, such a thing is clearly possible. Of its *a priori* probability or improbability we are not perhaps very competent judges. There are many things which a prejudgment would lead us to expect, that in actual fact are not as were anticipated. Especially is this the case in reference to the things of God; here, our prejudgments are falsified continually, and in reference to Scripture no less than in reference to other things. If, for instance, we should *a priori* have expected that Scripture, if inspired, would be infallibly accurate and exact upon every little point; *a priori* we should have equally expected that the integrity and purity of its text would have been so watched over by a superintending Providence, as to be preserved throughout all time as free from error as when it was first penned. But we know that it has not been so watched over; that errors of various kinds have changed it; that that which has happened to all other books has happened to the Bible also; that the text, in short, is, in certain places, more or less corrupted from what it originally was; and what is more, that in many cases it is obviously inaccurate and conflicting.

It has been said that the preservation of the text from all error would have demanded miraculous intervention, and that miraculous intervention was a thing not to be expected. Cannot God bring about a designed result otherwise than by miracle? Can he accomplish a purpose only miraculously? If so, then (miracles having ceased) his agency no longer begets events, no longer effects purposes, no longer answers prayer, no longer rules the world. Without miracle he has watched over and preserved the Scriptures themselves from perishing; and without a miracle he could, had he seen fit, as easily have preserved the sacred text from corruption; but he has not.

Again, *a priori*, we should have expected that all translations of Holy Scripture would have been divinely preserved from at least all material error. Has this been done? It has not. Could it not have been done? It could. Without miracle? Yes, without miracle.

A priori, we should have expected (since one at least of the ends contemplated by Scripture was the enlightenment and instruction of those who desired to know God's will) that God would have preserved his church from all misconception as to what was inspired Scripture and what was not. But not even this has been done. To say nothing of the conflicting opinions upon this point in our own day, what difficulties did not the early Christian church experience in this respect, and how discrepant were the conclusions of those who gave themselves to the inquiry—some receiving as Scripture only those books which the Jews themselves acknowledged, as Melito (A.D. 170), Epiphanius (A.D. 368), Jerome (A.D. 380), and Rufinus (A.D. 390); others inclining to the opinion that all the Greek additions of the LXX version were of equal authority, equally divine; and others holding this opinion in reference only to some of them. Cyril (A.D. 350), for instance, recognises only Baruch, with its appendix, the Epistle of Jeremiah; as does also the Council of Laodicea (A.D. 360). Origen (A.D. 230) rejects all these Greek additions, except the Epistle, as does also Hilary (A.D. 254). "But," says Hilary, "to some it seems good to add Tobit and Judith." Augustine (A.D. 400), together with the Councils of Hippo and of Carthage (A.D. 397), accept not these only, but the Books of Wisdom, Ecclesiasticus, and the Maccabees as well; whilst Jerome and other of the Fathers, together with the Church of England and Protestants generally, reject them all.

A priori expectations, then, in reference to Scripture, may be, have been falsified. Why, then, may not those which lead us to anticipate that if Scripture be inspired in one respect, viz., in a religious, it will be equally inspired in all?

In itself considered, it is clearly possible that a certain amount of small inaccuracies upon matters of no religious importance should co-exist with infallible accuracy in reference to religious truth; and whatever may be men's *a priori* expectations upon the matter, we will not undertake to say that the expectation that they would not co-exist, has not been as much falsified by fact, as those others adverted to above.

God's proceedings in reference to revelation have failed to realize *a priori* expectations in other particulars also, besides those already noticed; viz., in that it is not universal; in that upon some points it is incomplete, upon others obscure; and the like. Why then may not expectation have been falsified in this as well? "Since upon experience," says Bishop Butler, who has a chapter upon the subject,* "the acknowledged constitution and course of nature is found to be greatly different from what before experience would have been expected; it is beforehand highly credible that the revealed dispensation will likewise be found to be very different from expectations formed beforehand." The Bishop's illustrations of his argument are,

* "Analogy," part ii. chap. 3.

we think, very forcible. His "Analogy" is in every one's hand; let the reader turn to them.

Men may, if they please, make this absence of things expected by them, a reason for rejecting Scripture—some do. But the fact referred to by Butler as to God's proceedings in nature, may well cause us to suspect that such may also have been his proceedings in reference to revelation.

As regards the Book of Esther, the absence in it of a religious tone and spirit is particularly striking, and seems hardly to consist with the supposition of its being an inspired document. "The other sacred writings of the Jews," says Stuart, "represent God not only as the theoretical, but as the practical sovereign of the universe, dispensing both good and evil. Not so the Book of Esther. Omitting, as it does, all reference to an overruling Providence, it shows how transformed as to this style of thinking and writing the writer had become by living in a foreign country. The fasting and weeping (chap. iv.) betoken indeed a sense of religious dependence; and in iv. 14 there is an evident allusion to the promises of preserving the Jewish nation, let the danger be what it might.

But, whatever the writer's reasons were for an uniform silence on the subject of religion and divine interposition, he has not given them to us, and it is certainly with no small difficulty that we can make out reasons satisfactory to our own minds."—" Defence of the Canon," p. 161.

Dr. Davidson, as might be expected, puts this matter yet more strongly.

" The Jews were delivered from an undeserved and indiscriminate destruction by means which human forethought could not have devised. Their salvation was almost miraculous. Instead of being slaughtered by their enemies, their enemies were put to death by them. The history is pregnant with the manifestations of an overruling Providence, yet there is no recognition of the Supreme One to whom they owed their preservation. No gratitude is expressed for his favour. Indeed, there is an entire suppression of the religious spirit; the events being described in the cold manner of a secular writer whose philosophy rises no higher than the outward phenomena around him."—" Introduction to the Old Testament," ii. 166.

Its authorship has been variously conjectured. Our own belief (and it is, we believe, the only one which will satisfactorily account for its utter want of religious tone and spirit) is that advocated by the late Mr. Horne, viz., that it is a "translated extract from the memoirs of the reign of the Persian monarch Ahasuerus. The Asiatic sovereigns, it is well known, caused annals of their reigns to be kept, and the book itself attests that Ahasuerus had such records. Now, if it was necessary that the Jews should have a faithful narrative of their history under Queen Esther, from what more certain source could they derive such history than from the memoirs of the king, her consort? Either Ezra or Mordecai had authority or credit enough to obtain such an extract. In this case, too, we can better account for the retaining of the Persian word *Purim*, as well as for the details which we read concerning the empire of Ahasuerus, and for the exactness with which the names of his ministers and of Haman's sons are recorded. The circumstance of this history being an extract from the Persian annals will also account for the Jews being mentioned only in the third person, and why Esther is so frequently designated by the title of Queen, and Mordecai by the epithet of 'the Jew.' It will also account for those numerous parentheses which interrupt the narrative, in order to subjoin the illustrations which were necessary for a Jewish reader; and for the abrupt termination of the narrative by one sentence relative to the power of Ahasuerus, followed by another relative to Mordecai's greatness. Finally, it is evident that the author of this extract, whoever he was, wished to make a final appeal to the source whence he derived it (x. 2, 'Are they not written?' &c.). This very plausible conjecture, we apprehend, will also satisfactorily answer the objection that this book contains nothing peculiar to the Israelites except Mordecai's genealogy. There is, unquestionably, no mention made of Divine Providence or of the name of God in these memoirs or chronicles; and if the author of the extract had given it a more Jewish complexion—if he had spoken of the God of Israel—instead of rendering his narrative more credible, he would have deprived it of an internal character of truth."—"Introduction to the Holy Scriptures," edit. 7, iv. pp. 65, 66.

Whether the non-religious tone of the book be or be not a valid objection to its being of inspired authorship, we do not pretend to determine. But upon the supposition that it is, it must be borne in mind that the disproof of the inspiration of any one or more of the several books of the Old Testament as we now have it, in no respect invalidates the proof of the inspiration of the rest. The alternative is not either to receive in the mass or to reject in the mass. People in general are accustomed to believe that it is; that the canon, as it is called, has been authoritatively determined; and that no reasonable doubt exists that the whole of the books that were recognised as inspired and divine by Josephus, Melito, and others, were so recognised also by our Lord, and by the Jews of our Lord's time; and it is mainly from this consideration that Stuart, in spite of the difficulties to which we have adverted, and which he confesses to be embarrassing, maintains their right to be accepted as inspired.

But this is not the case. The only writings of the Old Testament that can with certainty be proved to have been recognised by our Lord as Scripture, are "The Law, the Prophets, and the Psalms" (or, according to the briefer and more usual formula, as in Matt. vii. 12; xi. 13; xxii. 40, &c., "The Law and the Prophets"[*])—

[*] The Psalms, by an understood conventionalism, being of course included. *See* Luke xxiv. 44, and Acts ii. 30.

these, and no other. There may be some difficulty in ascertaining with certainty the books that are included in this phrase; but, be they what they may, they and they only are the books recognised by our Lord as Scripture.

By "the Law," we understand, of course, the Pentateuch, or five books called the Books of Moses; all of which are repeatedly quoted in the New Testament, or referred to, as of divine authority.* But what books are to be

---

* Within certain limits, the inspiration of the Pentateuch is in no respect affected by the authorship either of Genesis or Deuteronomy. It is quite possible that the former was, strictly speaking, not so much written by Moses as collected and edited by him; and the latter, though spoken by him, may have been committed to actual writing, not by Moses himself, but by a contemporary, perhaps Joshua. Who actually wrote it, is, however, not material. It is referred to in the New Testament as having been at least *spoken by* Moses, and for us that is sufficient. For this reason, and for others also, we feel sure that at least Jeremiah did not write it.

As regards Bishop Colenso's other fancy, viz., that the other portion of the Pentateuch was written "probably by Samuel," a well-known writer who has taken no part whatever in the recent controversy, Dean Milman, makes a remark that, considering the quarter from which it comes, is extremely gratifying. "A recent view," says the Dean, "assigns the Pentateuch to the age of Samuel. This appears to me by no means a happy conjecture. Among the most remarkable points in the record in Exodus is its intimate and familiar knowledge of *Egypt*. All the allusions, with which it teems, to the polity, laws, usages,

included in the second of these divisions, viz., "the Prophets," must, to a great extent, be a matter of almost mere conjecture. It comprises of course the Prophetical Writings commonly so called (Isaiah, Jeremiah, &c.); and, as throughout the whole of the theocracy, from the days of the patriarchs down to the days of the last of the prophets, there appears to have been an uninterrupted succession of divinely enlightened and therefore of divinely inspired men, perhaps most of the historical books. Samuel, together with the prophets or seers, Gad, Nathan, Iddo, Isaiah, and Shemaiah, are expressly spoken of as having written more or less fully the histories of their respective times; so that whether those

---

productions, arts, to the whole Egyptian life, with which we have lately become so well acquainted, are minutely and unerringly true. Even the wonders are Egyptian, and exclusively Egyptian.

"But for the two or three centuries between the Exodus and Samuel, all intercourse with Egypt seems to have been entirely broken off. Between the Exodus and the Egyptian wife of Solomon (excepting an adventure with an Egyptian slave, in David's wars) there is no word which betrays relation to Egypt. During the Judges the Israelites are warred upon and war with all the bordering nations, but of Egypt not a word. The writer of that book, as well as of those of Samuel, seem even as if ignorant of the existence of such a country."—"History of the Jews," third edition, vol. i., Preface, p. xxvii.

which we have of those times are or are not those very histories, it cannot be doubted that they were, at the least, compiled therefrom. One of these books, viz., the First Book of Kings, is, upon one occasion, expressly quoted as "Scripture" ("Wot ye not what the Scripture saith of Elias?" &c.—Rom. xi. 2); and the histories of all of them (those of Esther, Ezra, Nehemiah, and perhaps Chronicles excepted) are repeatedly more or less referred to in the New Testament as veracious and authoritative. We may therefore conclude that at least the Books of Samuel and Kings, probably also of Joshua, Judges, and Ruth, and possibly of Chronicles, and of Ezra, and Nehemiah also, were so regarded and so classed. The Book of Job likewise (to which Ezekiel and St. Peter both refer, and which St. Paul also apparently quotes—1 Cor. iii. 19) may be presumed to have belonged to this division, and perhaps the Book of Proverbs. It is thrice quoted in the New Testament, and that probably, though not expressly, as Scripture (viz., in Heb. xii. 5; 1 Peter ii. 8; Rom. xii. 20). It is true that the mere fact that it is quoted does not prove it to have been such;

and that some have objected, in reference to this book, that its maxims are to a great extent prudential rather than religious. Perhaps they are, perhaps they are not; let each man judge for himself. No authorized canon, no divinely inspired council, has any authority over our faith in the matter.

The third division, "the Psalms," so far as we have the means of knowing, contained, or seems to have contained, *only* the Psalms. It is easy to assert that this third division consisted of more books than one, the first (that of the Psalms) giving name to the whole of them; but the assertion is an assumption. It may be true, or it may not; but there is no evidence to prove it. All that one can feel sure of is that our Lord's recognition as Scripture, of "the Law, the Prophets, and the Psalms," was, of course, the recognition of all the books that rightfully belonged to the one or the other of these divisions; but whether the books assigned to them by Josephus of right belonged to them, or whether they did not, of this we cannot feel sure.

If it were, as Stuart asserts, and as indeed is commonly asserted, certain that the books recognised by our Lord as Scripture were identical with those recognised by Josephus, and by Melito and others who wrote *after* the destruction of Jerusalem, then indeed we should as Christians be bound, upon our Lord's authority, to receive them as such ourselves. But the assertion that they were identical is a mere assumption, and cannot be substantiated.

With a view to the proving that it cannot, and for a clear apprehension of the facts of the question, it is desirable, before proceeding further, to give in full, and in their very words, the evidence (furnished by Sirachides, by Philo, by Josephus, and by Melito respectively), which has been supposed to warrant the conclusion which we have ventured to call a mere assumption. The earliest, indeed the only evidence bearing upon the question prior to the time of Christ, is that of Sirachides, in whose Prologue to the Book of Ecclesiasticus we meet with the following expressions :—

"Whereas many and great things have been delivered unto us *by the Law, and the Prophets, and by others that have followed in their steps,*" &c. (δια τον Νομον και των Προφητων, και των αλλων κατ' αυτους ηκολουθηκοτων.)

"My grandfather, when he had much given himself to the reading *the Law and the Prophets, and the other books of our Fathers,*" &c. (και των αλλων πατριων βιβλιων.)

"The same things uttered in Hebrew, and thence translated into another tongue, have not the same force in them; and not only these things, but *the Law itself and the Prophets* (or Prophecies), *and the rest of the books* (ο Νομος, και αι Προφητειαι και τα λοιπα των βιβλιων), have no small difference when they are spoken in their own language."

The evidence supplied by the writings of Philo (who flourished about A.D. 40), occurs in his treatise "De Vita Contemplativa," where, speaking of the Therapeutæ, or Essenes, he says:—

"In every house is a sanctuary, which is called the sacred place or monastery, in which they perform the mysteries of a holy life, introducing nothing into it but the Laws and oracles predicted by the Prophets, and Hymns, and the other [writings] by which knowledge and piety are increased and perfected. (Νομους, και λογια θεσπισθεντα δια Προφητων, και Ὑμνους, και τα αλλα οις επιστημη και ευσεβεια συναυξονται και τελειουνται.) . . . Addressing themselves to the sacred writings," &c. "They have also writings of their elders," &c.

Then comes that of Josephus, who in his book against Apion (I. 8.), written about A.D. 100, *i.e.*, about 30 years after the destruction of Jerusalem, writes as follows:—

"We have not an innumerable number of books among us, disagreeing from and contradicting one another, as the Greeks have, but only twenty-two, which contain the records of all the past times, and which are justly believed to be divine. Of these, five belong to Moses. As to the time from the death of Moses till the reign of Artaxerxes, King of Persia, the Prophets who were after Moses wrote down what was done in their times in thirteen books. The remaining four books contain hymns to God and precepts for the conduct of human life. It is true our history hath been written since Artaxerxes very particularly, but it hath not been esteemed of the like authority with the former by our forefathers, because there hath not been an exact succession of prophets since that time."

The 13 books of the "Prophets" of this passage are, as is well known, commonly regarded as comprising—1, Joshua; 2, Judges and Ruth in one book; 3, the two Books of Samuel; 4, the two Books of Kings; 5, the two Books of Chronicles; 6, Ezra and Nehemiah in one book; 7, Esther; 8, Job; 9, Isaiah; 10, Jeremiah and Lamentations in one book; 11, Ezekiel; 12, Daniel; 13, the twelve minor Prophets, Hosea, &c., and the 4 of "Hymns and Rules of Life," the Psalms, the Proverbs, the Song of Solomon, and the Book of Ecclesiastes.

The testimony of Melito, Bishop of Sardis, who flourished about A.D. 170, as given by Eusebius in his "Ecclesiastical History" (lib. iv. c. 26), is as follows:—

"In the beginning of his preface, Melito gives a catalogue of the books of the Old Testament acknowledged as canonical. This we have thought necessary to give here literally, as follows:—

"'Melito to Onesimus, his brother, greeting. Since you have often requested, through the earnest desire that you cherish for the Word, that you might have a selection made for you from the Law and the Prophets, which has respect to our Saviour and the whole of our faith; and since, moreover, you have been desirous to obtain an accurate account of the ancient books, both as to their number and their order, I have taken pains to accomplish this. . . . . Making a journey, therefore, into the East, and having arrived at the place where these things were proclaimed and transacted, I there learned accurately the books of the Old Testament, which I here arrange and transmit to you. The names are as follows:—The five books of Moses (Genesis, Exodus, Leviticus, Numbers, Deuteronomy); then Joshua of Nun, Judges, Ruth, four books of Kings, two of Chronicles, the Psalms of David, the Proverbs of Solomon (also called Wisdom), Ecclesiastes, the Song of Songs, Job. Prophets: Isaiah, Jeremiah, the Twelve in one book, Daniel, Ezekiel, Ezra' [including probably Nehemiah]."*

Now it is obvious, from a comparison of the testimony of Josephus with that given by

* Counting the books as arranged by Melito, we find them only twenty-one in number, which lacks one of the number as given by Josephus. The Book of Esther has been thought to have been dropped by accident, and perhaps it was; but both Athanasius (A.D. 326) and Gregory Nazianzen (A.D. 370) also omit it.

Melito, that his Old Testament and the Old Testament as now printed, are, as regards the writings recognised, one and the same. The only difference is that he arranges them differently.

But it must be remembered that the book that contains the testimony of Josephus upon the point (viz., his treatise against Apion) was not written until after the destruction of Jerusalem, (a fact of which I cannot find that any defender of the common Hebrew canon takes the smallest notice,) when *all* that remained of ancient Hebrew literature (including that which, upon religious or national grounds, the Jews had been accustomed more or less to reverence, though not inspired) may have been overestimated; so that to assume that the whole of the books recognised by Josephus and the Jews of his time were recognised also by our Lord and by the Jews of his time, is clearly a mere begging of the question. We do not say that they were not, but that there is no proof that they were. So far as testimony goes, they may or they may not. If it be true that there is not in any of the books of the Old Testament as recognised by Josephus anything that is in any respect inconsistent with inspiration, they may have been the same; but if, on the other hand, any of them contain matter that is in any respect inconsistent therewith, then we may feel sure that they were not.

We may wonder that the canon, as it is called, should be in any respect a matter of uncertainty. But it is. We have no divine, no authoritative decision upon the point. The tradition, though there is no proof of its being of ancient date,* that after the return from Babylon, Ezra and others collected into one volume all the then existing sacred writings, may be quite true. There is no improbability in it. On the contrary, it is more probable, perhaps, than otherwise. But there is no proof, even upon the supposition that he did so collect them, that the books collected by him and his successors as "*sacred*," included the whole of the books that were received by Josephus as *sacred*. Judging from our Lord's often-repeated formula, it is quite as probable, or rather much more, that the books regarded as "sacred," were simply "the Law, the Prophets, and the Psalms"—not the Law, the Prophets,

* The earliest mention of it being that of the Talmud.

and the Psalms, "and rules of life," as in Josephus; not the Law, the Prophets, and the Psalms, "and the other writings," as in Sirachides and Philo; but "the Law, the Prophets (understanding the term as above), and the Psalms" only.

The other—the non-prophetical books—those referred to apparently by Sirachides and by Philo, and by them referred to expressly as "the other"—(by them so spoken of, therefore, as if they were distinct from and belonged to neither of the three divisions into which the Scriptures proper were divided)—may have been added indeed as a sort of appendage, and probably were: just as the Jews of Alexandria added to their Greek version of the Hebrew Scriptures the writings of the Greek Apocrypha; and just as the Church of England appends, to this day, to its printed Bibles, books which it believes to be uninspired. But though added, there is no ground whatever for supposing that they formed any part of Scripture proper; or were collected or appended as divinely inspired; or were regarded as such until the time of Josephus, *i.e.*, until after the destruction of Jerusalem.

If we are to infer from the fact of the whole

of these books being collected into one volume, that they were equally regarded as Scripture proper, we must infer from the equally certain fact that the LXX (a Jewish translation, be it remembered) contained the apocryphal books, that these apocryphal books were also regarded as sacred—and that by and in the time of our Lord, who uses this version. But if they (the apocryphal books) were not so regarded (although in this translation appended to and even intermingled with the sacred writings), it follows that in the Hebrew volume also, no less than in the Greek translation, books that, upon religious or national grounds, were reverenced, though not inspired, may have been appended to books that were.

So long as "the Law, the Prophets (as that term was understood by the Jews, and by our Lord), and the Psalms," were alone recognised as Scripture—so long as non-Prophetical books were regarded as non-Prophetical, and non-Psalmistic as non-Psalmistic—no harm could result from their being appended, nor even from their being intermingled with them; any more than harm can result from the Bible and the Book of Common Prayer, or the Homilies, or Brady and Tate, being issued in one volume, and under one cover. The phrase defined as well as divided Scripture; so that mischief could arise only from a lax interpretation of it —only by so understanding it as to include under the one or the other of these divisions books that the definition did not comprehend— books that were not of the prophets among "the Prophets," and books that were not Psalms among "the Psalms."

There is (as we have already said) no evidence to show that this was done prior to the days of Josephus, *i.e.*, prior to the destruction of Jerusalem. These "other books" were reverenced, and cared for, and preserved, but there is no proof that they were ever regarded as *Scripture*, prior to his days—prior to that event. It is just possible that they may have been; we cannot venture to say that they were not; but we can venture to say that proof is wanting that they were.

But then, when Jerusalem had fallen, when its polity and worship were subverted, when its temple lay in ruins, then all that remained to the Jews of their ancient religious literature, whether inspired or not, would, we may presume, assume, in Jewish estimation, an increased importance. Books which up to this period had been preserved, not as inspired, but only as more or less valuable, those especially in which were preserved fragments of documents henceforth irrecoverably lost, they would, it is very likely, be disposed to over-estimate; and to receive, even as inspired, not only the hitherto recognised Scriptures of "the Law, the Prophets, and the Psalms," but all that remained to them of the writings of their ancient worthies—all those post-Babylonian fragments of their national history that were extant in their ancient native language, inspired or uninspired. Under these circumstances, and acting no longer under prophetic guidance, how natural then would it be that they should be disposed to incorporate with the Prophets and the Psalms of their Scriptures proper, those Hebrew books which hitherto may have been only appended to them?

The LXX having fallen into disrepute, in consequence, it is said, of the use made of it by the Christians, it is no wonder that they did not receive, as inspired, LXX contributions towards the history of their nation—the books of the Maccabees for instance; but those which were extant and ancient in their own language, and which custom had associated with their own Hebrew Scriptures, would naturally be very differently regarded by them.

Thus it is that we account for the reception by Josephus and his contemporaries, of books, as sacred and as inspired, which possibly were not inspired; and which there is no evidence whatever to show were ever regarded as such by our Lord, or in his time.

These other writings, moreover, are thenceforth (Jerusalem having fallen) no longer spoken of as "the other books," as by Sirachides and Philo; but classed, as we learn from Josephus, some with the Prophets, some with the Psalms. But this, the classification of his time, was temporary only; a subsequent one, that of the Masorites, transferring the books of Job, Ruth, the Lamentations, Esther, Ezra, Nehemiah, and Chronicles, together (strangely enough) with the Book of Daniel, to the latter of these divisions (to which in Josephus's time the writings of Solomon had already been appended), and changing the designation by which in our Lord's time this division was known, from "the Psalms," into that of "the Writings."*

And now comes the question, What are we to understand by the word "inspired," as applied to Scripture? Does it always indicate such suggestion or supervision—that unimportance, or incorrectness, or inexactness of statement, though of the most trivial kind, and upon subordinate and merely secular matters, are sufficient to disprove the inspiration of the

---

* The very fact that the classification of the Jews in the time of Josephus was supposed to need a revision, would of itself seem to indicate that this classification was not the original one, not that which was current in the time of our Lord, and which we may assume to have been of prophetic origin, and virtually, therefore, divine and authoritative; and so far, therefore, confirms, or seems to confirm, the opinion advocated in these pages as to the possible difference between the Old Testament of Josephus and the Old Testament of our Lord.

The changing also of the designation of the division known in our Lord's time as "The Psalms" (an appropriate designation if it contained the Psalms only), into that of "The Writings," upon the addition to it of writings that were not Psalms, and when, therefore, the appropriateness of the designation no longer existed, would seem also to confirm our yet further opinion that the third of the three divisions of our Lord's time included only the Psalms. With regard to the insertion in this division of the book of Daniel, see Stuart, p. 263; and for an admirable defence of its veracity and inspiration, see Walton's recently published "Genuineness of the Book of Daniel."

writing containing them? We have already said that we believe that it does not. If the writers of Scripture (whether in matters of petty and unimportant detail occasionally inexact or not) were, upon matters of religious truth, enlightened by God's Spirit above their fellows, so as to qualify them to make known to others, infallibly and authoritatively, the things of the Spirit of God, Scripture is certainly to that extent inspired; and if to that extent, sufficiently inspired for the purposes for which Scripture was given. If that which, in virtue of this enlightenment, they tell us respecting God and ourselves could not have been known to them apart from such enlightenment, or apart from express revelation, it follows, whether Scripture be or be not inspired in other respects, that it must be inspired in this. If that which it teaches us it teaches us not as a matter of opinion, but authoritatively, as that there is a God, that he is just, merciful, good, a moral governor, and the like—if it makes known to us his will, and to a certain extent his purposes, *authoritatively*, together with our obligations, our needs, and his provision for those needs; if it tells us *authoritatively*, how we may be saved, and how we may be lost; if it makes known *authoritatively*, that the body shall rise again, that there is a day of future and of righteous retribution, and that that retribution is eternal, unchanging, final—if it does this, it must, if it be inspired in no other respect, be inspired in this, viz., as regards religious truth.

Now it professes to do this, namely, to teach authoritatively, and our Lord recognises the claim; for he appeals to Scripture as conclusive, and therefore as being, as regards religious truth, inspired. Doubt, suspicion, disproof even, as to its inspiration in other respects, would be no disproof then of its inspiration in this.

Some of its statements upon religious points so commend themselves to our reason, that Reason not only accepts them, but thinks that she has, or could have, attained to the conviction of them by efforts of her own; though no people, either in ancient or modern times, unacquainted with the teachings of the Bible, has ever done so. But, upon the supposition that she could, it is manifest that she could not have attained to them all; for some of them rationalism rejects, as that God will so severely punish impenitence and sin, that he will save from such punishment only as there is faith in a provided Redeemer, and the like.

That which they make known to us respecting God is, for the most part, not that which naturally suggests itself to the human mind; nor when made known, is it that which men, without very much qualifying it, are at all disposed to receive. God's will is too much insisted on, and man's too little. No scheme of man's devising would have represented God, on the one hand, as so merciful, nor, on the other, as so severe as the Bible does; as offering to us the free forgiveness of all our offences, together with the renovation of our very nature, independently of any condition to be fulfilled on our part in the way of purchase or of atonement. No merely human scheme would have represented man as, in himself, completely lost; as incapable, by any striving or amendment of his own, to recover and save himself; as lying wholly at God's mercy. That the Bible method of reconciliation stands directly opposed to every scheme which human wisdom would have devised, is evident from the reluctance with which it is received, though revealed, and the objections by which it has been assailed. Naturally, men like rather to regard God as a God of mere love—as forgiving sin solely on the ground of pity, and out of indulgence to what are termed the weaknesses and imperfections of human nature. Men in general have no more idea of the perfection of God's mercy than they have of the perfection of his justice. They ascribe the salvation of sinners neither to the one nor to the other in perfection and in harmony, but in some way or other to the claims of both as mitigated by opposition. But the salvation of the Bible is of perfect justice as well as of perfect mercy, and of perfect mercy as well as of perfect justice; of perfect mercy, inasmuch as it declares salvation to be wholly of grace, without works of any kind as meriting or even as procuring it; and of perfect justice, inasmuch as in the rightful punishment of a willing substitute (for sin *demands* punishment—sin *ought* to be punished) law has been vindicated, and justice has had a full and more honourable vindication than it could ever have had in the punishment of the sinner himself. Human wisdom invariably expects either that God will not very severely punish sin; or else, if it take a sterner and juster view of sin's demerit, that exemption from deserved penalty is only to be expected so far as the sinner is or has something himself to merit it. The grace of God is not regarded as consisting in giving for nothing, but in giving at an under-value.

Upon these points, then, and such as these—points wherein the theology of Scripture differs from every other theology that has ever been accepted or conceived—we believe Scripture, all Scripture, to be clearly, truly, fully inspired; and he, in our opinion, is the happiest and wisest believer, and most correctly understands the word "inspired" as applied to Scripture, who (without very precisely defining the term, and without troubling himself with petty objections and petty difficulties that may or may not be valid, but that leave untouched and undisproved the divinity of its religious teachings) believes that the theology, the promises, the precepts, the doctrines of Scripture are all of them divine, all of them true, all of them to be depended upon, all of them authoritative, whether immediately suggested or not, whether directly dictated or not, and whether there be these objections and these difficulties or not. The word " inspiration " has been very variously defined;

but if this be believed, all is believed that can be known, and all is believed that is essential. A more precise definition is a mere speculation, a question ministering to strife rather than to edifying, a mere dogma that cannot be proved: and we doubt much whether St. Paul, in his well-known words to Timothy, ("All Scripture is given by inspiration of God, and is profitable for doctrine, for reproof, for correction, for instruction in righteousness; that the man of God may be perfect, throughly furnished unto all good works,") designed to affirm anything more definite.

For all practical purposes, the sufficiency of such an inspiration as this is undeniable; for, upon the supposition that the various books of Scripture were in any respect inspired (and that they were is assumed, and even asserted, by our Lord), for what end may we suppose them to have been so? Was it not that the church might, in all ages, have an infallible standard of religious doctrine to fall back upon?—that we might not be at the mercy of mere tradition? —that religious truth might be authoritatively, and divinely, and permanently stereotyped? If, then, the inspiration under which these books were written was an inspiration securing their writers infallibly from all error upon points of religious truth, shall we presume to doubt their inspiration because their writers were, or seem to have been, permitted to fall occasionally into some such petty misstatement upon points of unimportant detail as left untouched the substantial truthfulness and credibility of their various histories, and could be accounted for without impeachment of their integrity? Was it essential to the design contemplated by their inspiration that they should record, with rigid exactness, the precise locality and circumstances of Ahaziah's death; or whether the Syrians slain by David were horsemen or footmen; or whether Ahaz, when he died, was buried with his fathers or was not?

If inspiration were in all cases what it doubtless was in some, a simple, direct, immediate infusion into the minds of those whom we are accustomed to regard as inspired, both of matter and of words, then, if there be inexactnesses or discrepancies that cannot be reconciled, such inexactnesses and such discrepancies would of course, and at once, disprove their inspiration. They might be honest men, and, in the main,

E

truth-telling and trustworthy; but if infusion or dictation were the meaning, the necessary and sole meaning of the word, or if inspiration, in a religious respect, could not co-exist with non-inspiration in other and unessential respects, then it is clear that we must either be able to maintain that there are no such discrepancies, or give up, as disproved, the inspiration of their writings.

But under what necessity are we of so limiting the word, or of making any such supposition? God, in time past, spake no less in divers manners than at sundry times. If the writers of Scripture were so superintended as to be preserved from all error on religious points, and so directed and so influenced as to make known correctly and infallibly all religious truth, why should I doubt the inspiration of their writings because of certain small inexactnesses of unimportant detail, or why, on the other hand, claim for them an inspiration which they claim not for themselves—an inspiration securing them from all, even the least, discrepancy.

I know that if inexactnesses, however minute and unimportant, and though only occasional, be admitted, or, if admitted (for there are cases in which they must be admitted), be ascribed to any other cause than clerical error, the next step taken may be an inference that Scripture cannot be implicitly depended upon in any of its statements. But this next step, if it follow, follows as an abuse. It does not follow as a legitimate and necessary consequence. If there be honesty of purpose, however, mischief can scarcely arise from the belief that Scripture, though inspired, is not so inspired as to be in every respect the very word of God himself, unless that belief be held so vaguely that we cannot draw a line between that which, making known to us religious truth, we receive as inspired, and that which, being inexact or inaccurate, or the like, (for that is the hypothesis,) is manifestly human. Mischief may arise from the admission; but if there be discrepancy, inexactness, or inaccuracy, will none arise from their denial? will none arise from sophistical concealment? will none arise from forced, violent, improbable solutions?

But the question is not whether the admission may or may not be abused, but whether it be or be not demanded by the facts of the case, and whether, if it be, the inspiration of all Scripture must be given up in consequence. All truth is liable to abuse. The long-suffering and mercy of God, his willingness for Christ's sake alone to forgive all sin, the doctrine that we are justified not of works but by grace, the helplessness of man, the necessity of regeneration,— all truth may be abused, and is. He that desires to emancipate himself from the restraints of the word of God, may easily do so by means of a little sophistry, even though he should believe in the inspiration of every detail and of every word. But he who is honest of purpose—who seeks to know the truth, and to know and to do the will of God—how will his faith be endangered, if, admitting that there are or seem to be petty inexactnesses in some of the minor details of Scripture narrative, he nevertheless believes that, upon all points of religious truth, all Scripture is inspired? Nay, will he not even more heartily believe in the inspiration of Scripture in this respect, when he sees that the belief does not necessitate the reception, as inspired, of statements that conflict? He can now afford to admit the validity of many an objection against his favourite book, and yet still resort to it as being to him, as much as ever, the very book of books, the very truth of God. He will rejoice that its value as a standard of religious truth is altogether unaffected by matters that (even though admitted) detract in no respect from its worth as a religious guide, leaving its value in that respect unsullied and intact. He will feel that he may now hold fast the word of truth, without being at the same time compelled to fight, at a disadvantage, in the face of appearances, if not of facts—maintaining that to be no inaccuracy which he nevertheless secretly believes, or fears, or suspects to be one—anxious about the solution of every petty difficulty—uneasy if he cannot satisfactorily refute every small objection; for, holding fast to the conviction that the Bible is religiously inspired, he can even admit (should truth, or honesty, or probabilities demand it) the occasional inaccuracies, or inexactnesses of statement (such as they are) that may be alleged by scoffers against the book, together with many other matters equally irrelevant (that leave untouched the truthfulness of its religious teachings) that have been urged as objections; and yet feel that the admission would still leave the book, in religious respects, as much the word of God—as much the "inspired" word of God—as ever.

Men may shrink from this restriction of the applicability of the term "inspired" to the religious teachings of Scripture, as if it were dangerous. It shocks their preconceptions. They have been accustomed to regard every narrative, and every small detail of every narrative, as being equally inspired with every precept, every religious truth, every doctrine; and they cannot bring themselves to adopt any new opinion upon the subject. But it is not dangerous; it is safe. Their opinion is dangerous; for the question before us is not, Are there, or are there not, inexactnesses, contradictions, and the like? but, upon the supposition that there are such, Is the inspiration of Scripture to be given up? They say, perhaps, Yes, perhaps, No. If they say Yes, we deny it; if No, we too say No—but with this difference: according to them, the inexactnesses and the contradictions and the like are inspired; according to the opposite opinion, the inexactnesses and the contradictions and the like are not inspired. It is of no avail to say that there are not any; the hypothesis is, "*If* there be."

Incorrectness cannot have been inspired. Why then, if there be such, may not the inspiration of the writers of Scripture have had regard solely to the qualifying them to make known correctly and infallibly religious truth? Was it essential to the ends contemplated by it, that it should be characterized, not only by a rigid rightness of theology, and of religious sentiment, but by a rigid exactness of petty incident as well?

It is quite conceivable that God may have divinely preserved a writer from error where error would have been important; and not from error where error was not important. May he not even have permitted the petty inaccuracies (for the errors with which the narrative has been charged are nothing more) for probational ends—to test our disposedness to receive upon sufficient grounds as divine, the religious teachings of Scripture, which, upon the insufficient ground of certain unimportant inexactnesses, or some such small matter, in the histories in which those teachings are found, we might be tempted to believe to be merely human? Are we not, in reference to the things of God, continually thus tested? The goodness of God, the efficacy of prayer, the superintendence of God's providence—our belief in these, and a variety of other the like points, is based upon what we consider strong and sufficient evidence, but not upon evidence that is demonstrably conclusive; not upon evidence that is altogether free from difficulty; not even upon evidence against which opposing evidence may not be brought.

It is clearly the will of God that probabilities should content us in the affairs of ordinary life; and it seems no less clear that it is his will that probabilities should content us also in reference to the inspiration of Scripture. There is nothing unreasonable, then, or unlikely, in the supposition that it was agreeable to the wisdom of God that that which is substantially correct in the narratives of Scripture, and that the religious truths imbedded in them, should be mixed up with such unimportant inaccuracies, or seeming inaccuracies, or inutilities, or the like, as should suffice to form such an amount of uncertainty and of difficulty as would test our sincerity and candour.

Indeed, even upon the supposition that there

were no inexactnesses, no morally useless and religiously useless narratives, no stumblingblock of any kind, and that we received the Scriptures as throughout and in every respect inspired, we should still be obliged to fall back upon probabilities as to its teachings; for we can so prove from them as to be able to demonstrate, scarcely any one point, whether of doctrine or of duty. The divinity of Christ, for instance, might have been so asserted as, on Scriptural grounds, to admit of no debate. The perpetual obligation of the Sabbath; the mode of its observance; what upon that day was lawful, and what was not; the rights and duties of governments in reference to religious questions; the admissibility or the inadmissibility of infants to the ordinance of baptism; the lawfulness or unlawfulness of war;— these, and many other such points (respecting which men who alike accept Scripture as their rule, differ in sentiment), might have been so stated as to render all doubt respecting them impossible. But God has willed otherwise. Our belief, consequently, upon religious, no less than upon many other points, is almost always a belief in probabilities; so much so, that if not content with probabilities for our guidance, we must either drift along without any guide at all, or else, resigning the duty of investigation, and of using to the best of our power the divine gifts of reason and of judgment with which we have been endowed, recreantly delegate, sluggard-like, our duties and our rights in these respects to others, and submit ourselves to the guidance of whatever church or party may chose to call itself infallible.

Let it not be thought that there is danger only in rejecting, as uninspired, books that are inspired. If it be dangerous to reject wrongfully, it is as dangerous, and may even be more so, to receive wrongfully. Take, for instance, the books of which we have been speaking. In rejecting them, we reject no doctrine, no religious teaching, that we do not find elsewhere in books that are of admitted inspiration. In accepting them, we accept books whose inaccuracies or inexactnesses are such that even apologists are sorely puzzled to account for them upon the supposition of the inspiration of those books—to say nothing of the absence of religious tone and spirit by which one of them, the Book of Esther, is so remarkably distinguished; or whose religious teaching, as in the case of the Song of Solomon, is so obscure, so uncertain, that men doubt to this day whether to regard it as a religious allegory or whether as an amatory poem; or, as in that of Ecclesiastes, so questionable, that even its defenders admit that "apparently sceptical sentiments are found in it" ("Stuart's Defence of the Canon," p. 338); and can harmonize with these sentiments their belief in its inspiration, only conjecturally.*

Now, upon the supposition that these books are not inspired, with what needless embarrass-

---

* *Viz.*, either by supposing that the book is dialogistic, and that one of the colloquists is a sceptic; or, as Stuart, by supposing that its writer "gives the tenor and drift of his cogitations *while he was in doubt,* thereby disclosing," says Stuart, p. 339, "*many a sceptical thought.*"

As regards the wisdom with which Solomon was gifted, whether it is to be considered as having been tantamount to an inspiration such as would qualify him to make known authoritatively and unerringly religious truth, is, we think, somewhat questionable. The narratives in reference to it, as given in the Books of Kings and Chronicles, would lead us rather to infer that the wisdom asked for was simply political or judicial wisdom. "Give thy servant," such is the prayer, "an understanding heart *to judge thy people;*" "Wisdom and knowledge, *that I may go out and come in before this people:* for who can judge this thy people, that is so great?" (1 Kings iii. 9; 2 Chron. i. 10.)

ments does championship in their defence encumber us; and, failing to prove their inspiration to the satisfaction of the sceptic, who doubts not respecting these books only, but respecting all Scripture, how readily and naturally will the inference be made by him, that the inspiration of all Scripture is equally indefensible. This is the certain consequence of an attempt to defend at all risks.

While maintaining then the inspiration of all those books which our Lord clearly acknowledged, how much safer is it to admit the possibility of the non-inspiration of the rest—to be non-dogmatical respecting them—and to admit that the *whole* of the books recognised by Josephus and those recognised by our Lord, were possibly not identical.

APPENDIX.

ON THE DISCREPANCIES AND CANON OF THE NEW TESTAMENT.*

The same arguments will apply to the New Testament as to the Old. It is true that discrepancy (we mean discrepancy in the sense of differing and conflicting statements) has often been imputed to it where no such discrepancy exists. As instances, we might refer to such apparently conflicting accounts as those given respecting the two thieves: St. Matthew and St. Mark representing them as alike railing upon our Lord, whilst St. Luke's account would seem to represent only one of them as doing so; the apparent difference between St. Matthew and St. Luke as to the time of the return from Bethlehem to Nazareth, St. Luke appearing to speak of our Lord's parents, Joseph and Mary, as proceeding, so soon as the mother was purified, at once to Nazareth, informing us that

* Condensed from a paper contributed by the writer, in 1854, to Dr. Kitto's "Journal of Sacred Literature," entitled, "Discrepancy and Inspiration not incompatible."

"when the days of her purification (*i.e.*, forty days from the birth, Lev. xii. 2—6) were accomplished, they brought him to Jerusalem, and thence returned to Galilee to their own city Nazareth;" whilst Matthew relates that they went direct from Bethlehem to Egypt, remaining there until the death of Herod, and that it was not until after his death that they returned to Nazareth.

Condensation, or amplification, as the case may be, will, however, sufficiently account for and vindicate all such discrepancies as these. Since, for instance, the ultimate abode of our Lord's childhood was not Egypt, but Nazareth, and since the episode of the flight into Egypt is altogether omitted by St. Luke, it was quite justifiable on the part of the latter, and as truthful as it was justifiable (and if condensation was intended, unavoidable), so to speak of the movements of our Lord's parents as to represent them as passing, as if directly, from Jerusalem or from Bethlehem to Nazareth. And so, also, in the case of the two thieves. In the course of the three hours during which they and He who hung between them were living and suspended, there may have been the united reviling, but then there may also have been, on the part of one of the two, the subsequent repentance and rebuking, and on the part of the other mocking and obduracy up to the very last. St. Luke does not say that this was not the case; nor is his account at all inconsistent with the supposition that it was. Confining himself to a single circumstance, and to a single point of time, there was no need that he should relate in detail all that had occurred previously.

But there are instances in which their varied accounts cannot be so easily disposed of. St. Matthew, for instance, in the account given by him of the circumstances connected with the crossing of the lake of Gennesaret, having informed us (viii. 18) that "when Jesus saw great multitudes about him, he gave commandment to depart to the other side," proceeds as follows :—

"And a certain scribe came and said unto him, Master, I will follow thee whithersoever thou goest. And Jesus saith unto him, The foxes have holes, and the birds of the air have nests, but the Son of Man hath not where to lay his head. And another of his disciples said unto him, Lord, suffer me first to go and bury my father. But Jesus said unto him, Follow me, and let the dead bury their dead. And when he was entered into a ship, his disciples followed him" (Matt. viii. 19-23).

Whereas, by St. Luke, the declaration on the part of one of our Lord's hearers or disciples, that he would follow him whithersoever he went, together with the same reply ; and the request on the part of another, that he might be suffered first to go and bury his father, are represented as having occurred at a much later period, and upon a totally different occasion— being by him (St. Luke) related as having taken place, not on the borders of the lake of Gennesaret, but *in Samaria*, and as our Lord and his disciples were journeying to Jerusalem.

"And it came to pass when the time was come that he (Jesus) should be received up, he steadfastly set his face to go to Jerusalem, and sent messengers before his face: and they went, and entered into a village of the Samaritans, to make ready for him. And they did not receive him, because his face was as though he would go to Jerusalem. And when his disciples James and John saw this, they said," &c. "And they went to another village. And it came to pass, that, as they went in the way, a certain man said unto him, Lord, I will follow thee whithersoever thou goest. And Jesus said unto him, Foxes have holes," &c. "And he said unto another, Follow me. But he said, Lord, suffer me first to go and bury my father. Jesus said unto him, Let the dead," &c. (Luke ix. 51-60).

A circumstance not mentioned in St. Matthew's account is then added, viz., that—

"Another also said, Lord, I will follow thee; but let me first go bid them farewell which are at home. And Jesus said unto him, No man having put his hand to the plough, and looking back, is fit for the kingdom of God."

Various attempts have been made to reconcile these apparently conflicting accounts as to the time and locality of these sayings. By some—by Macknight, by Birks, and by Greswell, for instance—it has been supposed that on each of the two occasions spoken of, parties may have come forward and have addressed our Lord, and have been replied to as related; in other words, that the circumstance of the sayings in question, and of their replies, may have happened once and again.

Now it is quite conceivable that instances may have frequently occurred of individuals expressing a readiness to follow our Lord "whithersoever he went," and to such our Lord may have been accustomed to make the same reply as the reply here recorded. Instances may have occurred more than once also, of others excusing themselves when commanded by our Lord to follow him, upon the plea that an aged parent was still living, and perhaps dependent upon them for support; and they may have asked to be excused until after their father's death (for so it is that we understand the request "Suffer me first to go and bury my father"); and to them our Lord may possibly have been accustomed to give always one and the same reply. But we can scarcely think it at all probable that incidents such as these should have twice occurred in pairs. The suspicion, therefore, will suggest itself, and that in spite of our every effort to repress it, that either the one evangelist or the other has recorded the circumstances in question in a wrong connection.

We do not, we dare not, say that such is the case, but we do dare to say that such seems to be the case. But be it so; be it that either the one evangelist or the other has assigned to these sayings a date and a connection which do not belong to them. Not only is the fact that these circumstances are, or seem to be, differently reported, a proof, in addition to a multitude of others, of the absence of all collusion; but neither is the inspiration of either of these evangelists, if we understand the term inspiration in the sense attached to it in our previous pages (viz., as having reference solely to the qualifying of those inspired to impart correctly and authoritatively *religious* truth), at all affected by the difference.

F

Perhaps a more obvious instance of inaccuracy is that where Stephen, in his defence before the Council of the Jews, says:—

"So Jacob went down into Egypt, and died, he, and our fathers, and were carried over into *Sychem*, and laid in the sepulchre that *Abraham bought* for a sum of money *of the sons of Emmor, the father of Sychem*"—

confounding together two separate purchases—viz., that of the sepulchre purchased by *Abraham* of *Ephron, the Hittite*, at or near *Hebron*, where *Jacob* was buried (Gen. xxiii. 3—20, and l. 13), and that of a field at or near Shechem, or *Sychem*, purchased of the sons of Emmor, by, not Abraham, but *Jacob*, in which *Joseph* was buried (Gen. xxxiii. 19; Josh. xxiv. 32).

But here again, the error, if there be one—which seems unquestionable—(*see* Alford *in loc.*) is of no religious importance at all. Upon the supposition, then, that it is one, the inspiration of the discourse or book containing it, in a religious respect, remains as before. Discrepancies or inexactnesses such as these may serve to disabuse us of the opinion that the historical books of Scripture are verbally inspired, but as regards the religious inspiration of those books, they prove nothing either way. Their existence then may be admitted without detriment to the inspiration of the books containing them; and it is, we believe, wiser and more honest to grant their existence, at least in cases such as the above, than to labour to disprove them by violent and improbable interpretations, such as no Protestant apologist would admit to be valid;

if the conflicting, or seemingly conflicting statements, were found in the Maccabees or Tobit, instead of in the Gospels or the Acts.

A few words respecting the canonicity, as it is called, of the books of the New Testament, and we have done.

As there is no satisfactory evidence to show that the canon of the Old Testament was ever determined authoritatively, so neither is there any evidence to show that that of the New Testament was ever so determined. All that evidence can do is to supply us with the sentiments of the early church in reference to its several books, leaving us to infer therefrom according to the best of our ability. It is satisfactory to know that most of its books have been universally received by the early church as genuine and as inspired from the very first. But others of them, viz., the Epistle to the Hebrews, together with the Epistle of St. James, the Second Epistle of St. Peter, that of Jude, the Second and third of John, and the Book of the Revelation, as we learn from Eusebius, and from other sources, were not so received; and it is right that this difference as to the evidence upon which our reception of its several books is grounded, should be known.*

---

* Respecting the Epistle to the Hebrews, the testimony of Eusebius varies. *See* " Hist. Eccles.," iii. c. 25, 38, and vi. 20.

Why the early churches doubted, except in the case of the Book of Revelation, is not known; but in modern times doubts have been entertained respecting five of these books, upon the ground of their respective contents. Whether justly or not, is another question; that, each one must determine for himself as he best can. It is not possible to discuss the grounds upon which they have been severally rejected or received, within the brief limits of an Appendix; nor does such discussion fall within the design contemplated by these pages. All that an adherence to our main object permits us to observe is, that as is the Old Testament so is the New a collection of many writings; that these many writings are not equally attested; and that disproof or doubt in reference to any one or more of them, leaves unaffected the credibility and value of the rest.

We are so accustomed to the Bible as a whole, and to its two divisions—the Old Testament and the New Testament—as wholes, that we forget, or do not adequately realize, the fact that it is not one writing, but many writings— not one book which must stand or fall in its entirety, but many books, variously and unequally attested. This being a fact, it is right that it should be known and remembered—not forgotten or ignored. It may be abused, as all facts may; but it need not be. It may, on the contrary, be advantageously remembered and made use of; and, being a fact, those conclusions (whatever they may be) are more likely to be correct that are based upon it, than those that are formed in ignorance of it, or in forgetfulness. The natural tendency of the knowledge of facts is, not to lead to false conclusions, but to right ones.

But, after all, let us not forget that right conclusions and intellectual certainty in reference to Scripture is a thing of little consequence (or rather, of none at all) if there be not at the same time a cordial reception of its truths, and a firm determination, as God shall help us, to live on them, and by them, and to act them thoroughly out. A merely speculative faith is a thing of small value.

Extract referred to in Note, page 11.

"Theological triflers, who keep the truth at arm's length from their own conscience, for subtle and curious speculation alone, too often fall under the edge of the solemn warning—'From him that hath not, even that he hath shall be taken away.'

"There may be a stage, however, in the course of serious and thoughtful inquirers, in which their faith in the gospel itself is unshaken, but their traditional trust in the Bible is sorely tried, and in some measure gives way. With growing thought and knowledge, difficulties once overlooked start out into sudden relief, and may seem for a time to be insurmountable. They have been accustomed from childhood to hear the Bible spoken of as one book, the Word of God.

They examine it more closely, and find that it consists of many works, written by many different writers at remote periods of time, and bears traces, in every part, of its human authorship, in language, grammar, idiom, style, historical features, and even, in some cases, in doctrinal tone. They have been accustomed, again, to hear it defined by entire freedom from all error. But they find that errors of translation, errors of transcription, and readings probably defective, though comparatively slight in amount, are admitted almost universally by well-informed scholars, to exist within its pages; so that the ideal perfection, once ascribed to it, seems to disappear. They find numbers here and there which seem plainly to need emendation; and details, which appear more or less contradictory in different accounts of the same event. Quotations from the Old Testament in the New do not seem always strictly to correspond, even in words; and the meaning assigned, in some cases, does not appear, on the first glance, to be the natural and genuine interpretation. Again, large portions in some of the books of the Old Testament seem to be useless details, that bear no stamp of divinity, and are difficult to reconcile with the theory of a direct, miraculous, and all-perfect inspiration. These perplexities, when they first dawn upon the young Christian student (without, perhaps, destroying or sensibly weakening his faith in the gospel itself), may induce him to imitate the Alexandrian mariners when they cast out the wheat into the sea to lessen or avert the danger of a total shipwreck. The plenary inspiration of the Scriptures may then be regarded as a superstitious accessary, a needless incumbrance of the Christian faith, which, in an hour of peril, and out of love to that faith itself, it may be [thought] needful to sacrifice and cast away.

"A looser faith in the inspiration of the *whole* Bible, when it arises from such causes, *ought not to be confounded with a settled spirit of unbelief.*"—"The Bible and Modern Thought." By the Rev. T. R. Birks. Page 204.

Note, supplementary to that given at page 43.

Whether we can perceive it or not, the laws of Moses, as they are called, being in strictness the laws not of Moses but of God himself, must of necessity be so characterized by consummate wisdom and strict rectitude as to prove thereby, more or less clearly, the divinity of their original. We believe that they are so characterized. This, however, is a large subject, and its illustration and defence would demand much space; especially as the writer differs from current opinions upon many points of detail. He must, therefore, reserve it for a separate volume, which, being to a great extent already written, he hopes to have ready for press in the course of a few months.

BY THE SAME AUTHOR.

THE PENTATEUCHAL NARRATIVE VINDICATED FROM THE ABSURDITIES CHARGED AGAINST IT BY THE BISHOP OF NATAL. Second Edition. 1862. 8vo. Price 8d.

BAGSTER & SONS, Paternoster Row.

THE INCREDIBILITIES OF PART II. OF THE BISHOP OF NATAL'S WORK UPON THE PENTATEUCH. 1863. 8vo. Price 8d.

BAGSTER & SONS, Paternoster Row.

www.ingramcontent.com/pod-product-compliance
Lightning Source LLC
Chambersburg PA
CBHW020306090426
42735CB00009B/1241